SPORTS GREAT ISIAH THOMAS

—Sports Great Books—

Sports Great Charles Barkley (ISBN 0-89490-386-1)

Sports Great Larry Bird (ISBN 0-89490-368-3)

Sports Great Roger Clemens (ISBN 0-89490-284-9)

Sports Great John Elway (ISBN 0-89490-282-2)

Sports Great Patrick Ewing (ISBN 0-89490-369-1)

Sports Great Bo Jackson (ISBN 0-89490-281-4)

Sports Great Magic Johnson (Revised and Expanded)
(ISBN 0-89490-348-9)

Sports Great Michael Jordan (ISBN 0-89490-370-5)

Sports Great Joe Montana (ISBN 0-89490-371-3)

Sports Great Hakeem Olajuwon (ISBN 0-89490-372-1)

Sports Great David Robinson (ISBN 0-89490-373-X)

Sports Great Darryl Strawberry (ISBN 0-89490-291-1)

Sports Great Isiah Thomas (ISBN 0-89490-374-8)

Sports Great Herschel Walker (ISBN 0-89490-207-5)

SPORTS GREAT ISIAH THOMAS

Ron Knapp

—Sports Great Books—

ENSLOW PUBLISHERS, INC.
Bloy St & Ramsey Ave.
Box 777
Hillside, N.J. 07205
U.S.A.

P.O. Box 38
Aldershot
Hants GU12 6BP
U.K.

Library of Congress Cataloging-in-Publication Data

Knapp, Ron.
Sports great Isiah Thomas / Ron Knapp.
p. cm. — (Sports great books)
Includes index.
Summary: Discusses the life and career of the basketball player who led the Detroit Pistons to a dominant position in the NBA in the late 1980s.
ISBN 0-89490-374-8
1. Thomas, Isiah, 1961– —Juvenile literature. 2. Basketball players—United States—Biography—Juvenile literature. 3. Detroit Pistons (Basketball team)—Juvenile literature. [1. Thomas, Isiah, 1961– . 2. Basketball players. 3. Afro-Americans—Biography.] I. Title II. Series.
GV884.T47K57 1992
796.323'092—dc20
[B]

91-41528
CIP
AC

Printed in the United States of America

10 9 8 7 6 5 4 3 2 1

Photo Credits: Boston Celtics, p. 41; Dallas Mavericks, p. 42; DePaul University, p. 20; Einstein Photo/Allen Einstein, pp. 9, 10, 13, 18, 33, 34, 36, 38, 46, 51, 54, 59; Indiana University, pp. 24, 25, 28; Los Angeles Lakers, p. 44; Michael Sargent, the White House, p. 57; MSU Broadcast/Marketing/Photo, Division of University Relations, p. 26.

Cover Photo: Einstein Photo/Allen Einstein

Contents

Chapter 1

The date was May 21, 1989 at the Palace of Auburn Hills—home of the Detroit Pistons, a professional basketball team. The Pistons and the Chicago Bulls were facing off in the first game of the Eastern Conference playoffs. Most of the attention was focused on two players—Chicago's Michael Jordan and Detroit's Isiah Thomas. Jordan was confident. "We'rc going to win," he told reporters. "And if we win the first game, we're going to win the series." The first team to win four games would advance to the National Basketball Association (NBA) championship finals.

Thomas also looked forward to the series. "There's nothing to match the high you get from competing in a game in front of a national television audience and 20,000 screaming fans." The 6-foot 1-inch Piston guard knew it was not going to be easy. "Michael Jordan," he said, "is virtually impossible to stop. You hope to slow him down and contain him, but that's about it." Detroit coach Chuck Daly called Jordan a "one-man wrecking crew."

Jordan wrecked the Pistons that day at the Palace. He

scored 32 points and grabbed 11 rebounds. In the second half the Bulls led by 24 points. The Pistons rallied, but still lost 91–88. Thomas played poorly. He made only 3 out of 18 shots. "I felt terrible," he said, "not only because of the way I played, but because I felt I had let the whole team and the whole organization down."

The Pistons came back in the second game, and this time Thomas was the wrecking crew. He scored 33 points to help Detroit win 100–91, but he was not satisfied. "I still don't like the way we're playing as a basketball team. We're not playing well enough to win this series." In this second game Jordan had the flu, but he still was able to score 27 points.

Isiah and the Pistons began the third game by playing their best basketball of the series. With seven minutes left in the game, they had a 14-point lead. Then Michael Jordan took over. He scored 17 fourth-quarter points. The game was now tied 97–97 with just 28 seconds left. Detroit had possession of the ball and called a timeout. Coach Daly tried to explain a play, but the Pistons could barely hear him over the roar of the excited Chicago crowd.

Bill Laimbeer, Detroit's six-foot 11-inch center, interrupted the coach with his own idea. "Give the ball to Isiah," he yelled. "Isiah's the one who got us here, and he'll be the one to win it for us."

Daly was not sure that was a good idea. "But he's got Michael Jordan on him," he said.

"Forget Jordan," Laimbeer replied. "We need to win this game and Isiah's the one to do it." Daly finally agreed.

Thomas got the ball and watched the seconds tick off the clock as he dribbled, waiting to take his shot. Laimbeer positioned himself between Jordan and the basket. He wanted to screen the Chicago superstar so Isiah could get free for the shot. Laimbeer and Jordan bumped into each other and the

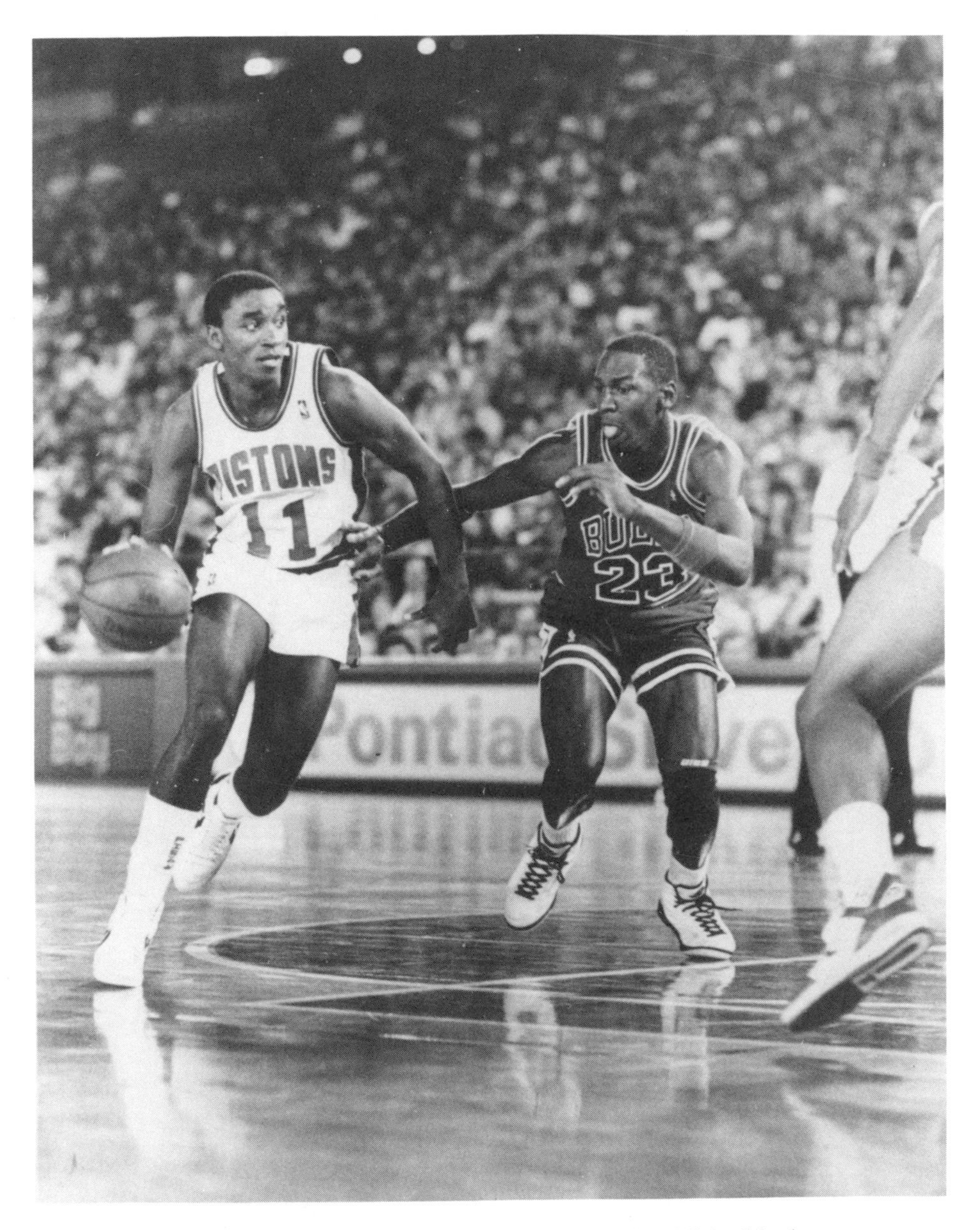

Isiah tries to make a move toward the basket against Michael Jordan.

referee blew his whistle. Laimbeer had been called for an offensive foul. The game was still tied, but now Chicago had the ball with nine seconds left.

Nobody was surprised when the Bulls passed the ball to Jordan. He drove down the right side of the lane. Dennis

Isiah prepares to shoot a free throw.

Rodman of the Pistons was there to guard him. Thomas shifted over so that Jordan was double-teamed. With three seconds left Jordan jumped up in the air. So did Rodman and Thomas to try and block the shot. The ball hit the backboard and bounced in. The Bulls won 99–97.

Now the Pistons were in trouble. They were down two games to one. If they lost just twice more their season was over. And their dream of an NBA Championship would be finished. Isiah knew the next game would be significant. "I looked at this game as maybe the most important game of my career," he said. "Everything was on the line."

The Pistons knew they had to stop Jordan. Daly reminded his players of the "Jordan Rule." A reporter later asked Daly what the rule was. "Whenever he goes to the bathroom," the coach joked, "we all go with him." He wanted the Piston players to stick with Jordan all over the court. Every time Jordan had the ball, two or even three Pistons were supposed to be guarding him. Thomas was confident the Jordan Rule was finally going to work. Before the fourth game he told Daly, "I guarantee you the Bulls aren't going to score more than 80 points tonight."

Isiah was right. The Piston defense held tight. With less than two minutes to go, Detroit led 82–76. But the Bulls were not out of it yet. When Michael Jordan is playing against you, a six-point lead is not much. Thomas's team was counting on him. "We told him that he had to do it because he is the man," said teammate John Salley. "We needed him today like never before, and he led us like he knows how."

With 90 seconds left Chicago's Horace Grant tried to go up with a shot that would have cut Detroit's lead to four. But Thomas stole the ball right out of his hands, and the Piston lead held. Detroit won 86–80, and the series was tied at two games apiece. "Thomas was everywhere," the *Detroit Free Press* reported. He had 27 points and 10 rebounds.

Detroit then defeated the Bulls 94–85 and 103–94 to take the series. The Pistons had obeyed the Jordan Rule. "At times, the way the defense is playing me," Jordan said, "it does feel like being handcuffed." The Pistons did not spend much time celebrating. "This is nice," Thomas said, "but we want an NBA championship. We don't have that yet." They still had to face the Los Angeles Lakers, the team that had beaten them in the finals the year before. In 1988 the Pistons had come within a game of taking the NBA championship. In 1989 they wanted to win it all.

In the first game against Los Angeles, Thomas began the scoring with an easy jump shot. "Once that first shot went in," he said later, "I knew . . . that there was no way the Lakers would beat us." In fact, the Pistons could not be stopped. They defeated the Lakers 109–97. Isiah finished with a game-high 24 points.

In the third quarter of the second game Isiah watched his friend Earvin "Magic" Johnson hobble off the court with a pulled hamstring. Even without Magic, though, Los Angeles led 92–84 going into the final quarter. Detroit battled back to take a 106–104 lead with 32 seconds remaining. The Pistons ran the clock down to 8 seconds. But then they lost the ball because they could not get off a shot within the required 24 seconds.

James Worthy of the Lakers took the ball, but was fouled by Rodman before he could shoot. If Worthy made his two free throws the game would be tied. There were two seconds left. Isiah stood waiting for the rebound and whispered to himself, "Please miss it, please miss it." He got his one wish. Worthy's first shot did not go in. After Worthy made the

Vinnie Johnson, Joe Dumars, Dennis Rodman and John Salley were Isiah's teammates during the Pistons' championship seasons.

second shot, Thomas was fouled. He sank both of his free throws, and the Pistons won 108–105.

Joe Dumars was the weapon for Detroit in the third meeting. Early on in the game he knew he was hot. "I don't care what plays we run," he told Thomas. "Just give me the ball." That is what Isiah did. Dumars wound up with 31 points, and Detroit got the victory 114–110.

The Lakers led early in the fourth game 42–26. But once again the Pistons stormed back. Detroit won the game, and the title, 105–97. After eight years in the NBA, Isiah Thomas was the captain of the world champions. "It was everything I had ever wanted," he told reporters.

But even before his team had taken the title, he knew he was a lucky man. "I'm living the dream I had since I was a little boy. How many kids, especially kids who grew up as poor as I did, ever live to see their dreams come true?"

Chapter 2

Isiah Lord Thomas III was born April 30, 1961 in Chicago, Illinois. He was the ninth and last child of Mary and Isiah Thomas II.

The family lived in a tough neighborhood on the west side of Chicago. The Thomases taught their children that it was important to stick together. According to Isiah's brother Preston, their father had a lecture for his seven sons. "He would gather seven sticks and put them in a bunch and tell us, 'It's a lot harder to break seven sticks together than one at a time.'" The streets were dangerous—filled with thieves, gang members, and drug dealers. The Thomas kids had to look out for each other.

When Isiah was a baby his father lost his job at a factory. After that the family was almost always short on money. Sometimes there was not even enough to buy food. Soon Mr. and Mrs. Thomas separated. Mary Thomas was left alone to raise her seven sons and two daughters.

"Some days I didn't have three meals to eat," Isiah said later. "But there was always plenty of love." Since he was the youngest his mother and the other children kept a special eye on him. They called him "Junior." "He was well behaved, but spoiled," his mother said. "He's still like that, spoiled rotten—by me and his brothers. They try to put the blame on me, and I can't say I didn't treat him special."

His family thought "Junior" was special. He was the baby of the family and he had an adorable smile. He was also a pretty decent basketball player. When he was just three years old he watched his brothers play in a Catholic Youth Organization (CYO) league. At halftime he walked onto the court and showed the crowd his stuff. "We gave Isiah an old jersey that fell like a dress on him," said Brother Alexis, one of the men who ran the league. "Isiah was amazing . . . At age three, he could shoot the eyes out of the basket."

But the Thomas brothers had more to think about than basketball. There were two rival street gangs in the neighborhood, the Mad Black Souls and the Vice Lords. One day, when Isiah was just 6, eight Vice Lords knocked on the front door. His mother answered.

"We want your boys," one of the gang members told her. "They're old enough to join us."

Mary Thomas was not about to let her sons join a street gang. "There ain't but one gang in this family," she told them. "The Thomas gang." The Vice Lords were not impressed. They refused to leave.

So Mary Thomas headed inside and came back with a sawed-off shotgun. "If you don't get off my porch," she yelled, "I'll blow you across the expressway."

The Vice Lords left. After that the gangs stayed away from Mary Thomas. "I wasn't scared of them," she said. "I stood up to them. They respected me." She kept her children out of the gangs. She also made sure they behaved themselves. If they misbehaved they knew they would be spanked.

Isiah once stole a plum from a small grocery store near his home. A security guard took him to a back room and said he was going to call the police. That was bad enough, but what really upset Isiah was when the man said he was first going to call his mother. "No!" the little boy cried. "Call the police, but please don't call my mother!" He knew what Mary Thomas thought of stealing.

When he got older his brothers took him to the outdoor court at nearby Gladys Park. They played there year-round. In the winter they brought shovels to clear the snow off the court. "That's where I really learned to play," Isiah said. Lord Henry Thomas, Isiah's big brother, was the star at Gladys Park. "Every move that Lord Henry made on the court, we'd try to duplicate it," Isiah said. "Oh, he was sweet!"

One of Isiah's friends was a neighborhood boy named Mark Aguirre. "We played in a 'bitty' league together," Aguirre said, "We were maybe nine years old." Years later he showed a reporter a doorway near the court. "That's where we would sneak out to get away from the gangs. They wanted our money. They knew we had to have 25 cents for the bus, so they came after us." If the gangs found them, Mark and Isiah gave up their quarters and had to walk home.

When Isiah was twelve, his family moved. The drug problem was getting worse, and the gangs were getting more violent. Mary Thomas decided the neighborhood was no place to raise a family. "When things started getting bad," she said, "I started moving." Their new home was five miles further west.

When he got older Isiah talked about life in his new neighborhood. "Those were probably the worst times as a kid. We very rarely had heat. We had an oil furnace but no money to buy oil. In the winter it was always cold and you had to sleep all the time with your clothes on. The staircase was falling down. The plumbing didn't work. I mean everything was a disaster." It was also crowded. Sometimes Isiah had to sleep on the floor of a closet. "A lot of times I slept on the ironing board in the hall."

Despite Mary Thomas's efforts, some of her older sons began to use drugs. Isiah thought about using drugs, too. That made his big brother Larry angry. One night he showed Isiah a bag of heroin. "This stuff will kill you," he said. Larry told Isiah to forget about drugs and concentrate on basketball.

"Out of all my brothers," Isiah said later, "he was the one who really saved me. At that time in my life I was lost. He started to spend a lot of time with me." Day after day Larry

Mary Thomas visits Isiah at a Pistons home game.

took Isiah to the basketball court and helped him improve his game. He told his brother he was going to be a star.

The Thomas brothers thought Isiah was a pretty good player. So did Gene Pingatore, the varsity basketball coach at St. Joseph High School. Isiah's eighth-grade team played a game in his gym. "I went there to watch a big 6-foot 4-inch kid," Pingatore said. "But as soon as Isiah hit the floor, he caught my eye. I knew he was special. Here was this tiny little kid dominating the game."

St. Joseph High School was in Westchester, Illinois—a wealthy suburb several miles from the Thomas home. Pingatore wanted Isiah to be a guard on his team. He offered him a scholarship because he knew Mary Thomas could not afford to pay his tuition. Isiah, his mother, and his brothers were very happy. They knew St. Joseph was a fine school. And they were sure Isiah would be a star on the team.

Even before the school year started, Isiah played with some of Pingatore's high school team in a summer league for adults. "Once we played some guys who were 19 and 20 years old," the coach said. "Even though he was just out of eighth grade, Isiah dominated the game. The other team got so frustrated, they wanted to fight. We almost had a riot."

Isiah had to leave home every day at 5:30 A.M. to make it to his new school on time. After an hour and a half on the city buses, he had to walk another mile and a half. His mother knew it was not easy for him. "I used to feel so sorry for him," she said. "I watched him leave and I cried."

Isiah almost did not make it through his first year at St. Joseph. He was playing great basketball, but his grades were terrible. He had a "D" average. "I'm doing OK," he told his coach. "I didn't come here to get good grades. I came here to play basketball." His mother and Coach Pingatore were not

Isiah's boyhood friend Mark Aguirre played basketball for DePaul University.

pleased. "We nipped that attitude in the bud," the coach said. "After his freshman year he was on the honor roll."

Isiah Thomas had a goal: he wanted to be a professional star in the NBA. To do that he had to play on a major college team. To get into a good college, he had to get noticed when he was in high school. To stay on the high school team, he had to get decent grades. If his grades were bad the whole dream fell apart.

"He was a kid who knew exactly what he wanted," said Pingatore. "He wouldn't let anything stand in his way. He is very focused. He had to get the grades to play basketball, so he just got them."

But Isiah also had a few things to learn about basketball. He was all over the court, not bothering to pass to the other players. He tried to do it all himself. Pingatore did not allow that. Every time Isiah took a bad shot the coach pulled him out of the game. "He was a little out of control," Pingatore said. "But the control he learned. It got to be when he took a bad shot, he didn't wait to get yanked. He just ran to the bench."

In Isiah's junior year the St. Joseph Chargers went 32–1, and finished second in the Illinois state high school tournament. The next year they were hoping to be the state champs, but something went wrong.

Even though Thomas was averaging 40 points a game, the Chargers lost two of their first three games. He and his coach had a talk. "Your 40 points are not what's needed to get the victory." Pingatore told him. "You've got to involve the other players. You've got to distribute the ball."

Isiah listened. His point total went down, but the victories started piling up. St. Joseph won 25 games in a row. The team looked like it was on the way to a state title. However, the season ended in the playoffs against De LaSalle High School. In this game the Chargers were defeated by a 30-foot jump shot at the buzzer. Thomas had fouled out and was already sitting on the bench. Years later he still says the De LaSalle game was the toughest loss he ever had. The St. Joseph Chargers never won the state championship.

Isiah's high school career ended. Now it was time to move on to the next part of his dream. Isiah had to choose a college—a difficult task, indeed.

Chapter 3

By the time he had finished his senior year at St. Joseph, Isiah Thomas was one of the most famous high school basketball players in the nation. More than 100 colleges wanted him for their team. They sent recruiters to watch him play and to talk to him and his family. "It was a zoo," said his high school coach Gene Pingatore.

All the attention did not seem to bother Isiah. Rick Majerus, an assistant coach at Marquette University, was one of the many men who tried to recruit Thomas. "He was a really genuine person." Majerus said. "The neighborhood was extraordinarily tough . . . . There was garbage strewn everywhere, a typical ghetto . . . . You'd go in there and here was this young guy who's got this big smile. He was unbelievably optimistic . . . . He was very focused."

The task of picking a college was not easy. When he was younger Isiah had dreamed of going to the University of Notre Dame. Pingatore suggested that he consider Indiana University because the school had a great coach, Bobby Knight. Mary Thomas and Isiah's brothers wanted him to attend DePaul University since it was just a few miles from their home. Also Isiah's friend, Mark Aguirre, was already playing for De Paul.

Some of the recruiters offered Isiah money or fancy cars if he would attend their particular school. Isiah listened to their promises and then made his own decision. He decided to go with Bobby Knight at Indiana. Mary Thomas was sorry that Isiah would be leaving home to go to college, but she liked Knight. "He didn't try to bribe me," she said. "Other schools offered hundreds of thousands of dollars . . . . All Bobby Knight promised was he'd try to get Isiah a good education and give him a good opportunity to get better in basketball . . . . I liked that."

Not everybody liked Bobby Knight, however. He is known for his quick temper. In fact, when he came to visit the Thomas home he almost got into a fight with Isiah's brother Gregory. Some people also did not like the way Knight treated

Isiah decided to attend Indiana University.

his players. They said he was mean and unfair. On the other hand, many other people think he is one of the greatest college basketball coaches of all time. Yet nobody can argue with Knight's statistics. His teams at Indiana almost always win. In 1976 the Hoosiers were undefeated national champions.

During the summer before he went to Indiana, Isiah had a chance to play for Knight. Isiah was on the United States team coached by Knight, in the 1979 Pan American Games in Puerto Rico. In one game Isiah got his first taste of the coach's temper. Knight did not like the way Thomas was playing. He threatened to send him home before the tournament was over. "You ought to go to DePaul, Isiah," Knight yelled, "because you sure as hell aren't going to be an Indiana player playing like that."

But Isiah stayed, and Knight was glad he did. Thomas helped the U.S. team win the championship. His passing was especially sharp. And he had more assists than anybody on the

Bobby Knight was Isiah's coach at Indiana.

Earvin "Magic" Johnson tries to move the ball past Indiana State University's Larry Bird in the 1979 NCAA Championship game. After leading Michigan State University to the title in his sophomore year. Johnson left college to become a professional player in the NBA for the Los Angeles Lakers. Bird didn't sign with the Boston Celtics until he had graduated from ISU.

team. In the title game against Puerto Rico, Isiah scored 21 points, and the U.S. team won 113–94.

Back home in Chicago, Isiah's family still called him "Junior." His friends such as Aguirre called him "Zeke." And when Isiah got to Indiana, Knight called him "Pee Wee." But Isiah did not mind. After all he was only 6-foot 1-inch, which was short for a college basketball player. Most of the time Thomas and Knight got along very well. Isiah knew his coach was making him into a better basketball player. Knight hoped that "Pee Wee" would help lead his team to another national championship.

The Indiana Hoosiers did not win the national title in 1979–80. Isiah's freshman year. But they were champs of the Big Ten with a 21–8 overall record. Thomas led the team in scoring (423), assists (159), and steals (62). He was named as one of the guards on the All Big-Ten team by the Associated Press. Isiah was the first freshman ever to receive that honor.

In Thomas's sophomore year he had his best game when scoring 39 points against Michigan. Indiana whipped Michigan 98–83. Once again the Hoosiers won the Big Ten title.

Isiah and his teammates were still hot when they hit the 1981 National Collegiate Athletic Association (NCAA) tournament. They advanced all the way to the title game against the North Carolina State Tar Heels. In this game Indiana fell behind 16–8. Four outside jumpers from Randy Wittman kept the Hoosiers in the game. By halftime Isiah had only made one shot from the floor. But Indiana had a 27–26 lead.

Thomas finally got rolling in the second half. He stole a pass at midcourt, then dropped in a layup. After a Tar Heel basket, he flipped a pass to Landon Turner who scored. Then with another interception and a basket, Indiana was up by five,

Isiah looks over the defense before making his move for the Hoosiers.

33–28. Soon Isiah had two more baskets and the score was 39–30. North Carolina was just about finished. Indiana finally won the game, and the 1981 NCAA title 63–50.

After the tournament Thomas was on the cover of the popular sports magazine, *Sports Illustrated.* The story poked fun at his big smile, "balloon cheeks," and boyish good looks. Isiah might have looked like a kid, but he certainly did not play like one. He was named the tournament's outstanding player, amassing 91 points and 43 assists in just 5 games. When it counted the most, in the title game, he had 23 points—more than any other player.

The coaches and sports reporters named him to several All-American teams. He was only a 19-year-old college sophomore, but he was already one of the most famous athletes in the country.

Now Isiah had another difficult choice to make. He could play two more years at Indiana. Or he could give up his college career and become a professional player in the NBA. Again, Isiah faced a tough choice. If he stayed at Indiana he could finish his college education, and perhaps, play on another championship team. If he went into the NBA he could sign a contract for hundreds of thousands of dollars. As a college player he made nothing. The Thomas family still lived in a rough dirty neighborhood on the west side of Chicago. They could certainly use the money.

After Isiah's great performance in the championship game, many NBA teams wanted him to play for them. Bobby Knight and his Indiana teammates waited to see what Isiah would do.

Chapter 4

Deciding whether or not to stay at Indiana was a tough decision. "There was a lot to consider," Thomas said. "I know I'm a role model for a lot of people back in the ghetto. Not too many of us get the chance to get out, to go to college. If I quit school, what effect would that have on them?"

Isiah had planned to get a degree from Indiana after four years and then attend law school. That was what Mary Thomas still wanted him to do. "I didn't want him to go pro," she said. "I wanted him to stay . . . and get his degree."

Finally Isiah made his decision. "I realized that I can always get an education," he said, "but I can't always get the cash." He announced he was leaving Indiana. In the June 1981 NBA draft he was the second player chosen—behind his old pal Mark Aguirre. Thomas went to the Detroit Pistons, while Aguirre was picked by the Dallas Mavericks.

Isiah signed a four-year contract with the Pistons that paid him $1.6 million. The first thing he bought was a beautiful house for his mother in Clarendon Hills, a suburb of Chicago. "Seeing her in that new house when she moved in—that probably is the most happiness, the most pleasure, I've had in my life," Isiah said. "Watching her going from having nothing to having something. When I go home I can walk to the refrigerator, and it's got food in it! That's happiness. We've got food in the house, and the bills are being paid!"

Mary Thomas loved the new house, but she wanted something else from her youngest son. "I made him sign a contract that he would finish school," she said. Of course, the contract was not legally binding, but she expected him to keep his promise. Even if Isiah was a rich professional athlete, she still wanted him to get his college education. She said he could take classes when he was not playing basketball. Most athletes forget about college when they sign professional contracts. But Mrs. Thomas said her son was going to be different.

Before he could think about classes, Isiah headed for Detroit. The Pistons were one of the worst teams in the NBA. They had never finished higher than second in their division. While Isiah and his teammates at Indiana were winning the national championship in 1981, the Pistons were struggling to a 21–61 record.

Scotty Robertson was the coach. It was not an easy job. "I used to lie in bed at night," he said, "and try to think of something positive to tell the players and the media." There was not much positive to say until Isiah arrived. Right away things started to change. With Thomas playing guard the Pistons won 8 of their first 13 games in 1981. And attendance at their home games almost doubled. The *Detroit News* called him "Isiah the Savior."

In his first month as a pro Thomas averaged 21 points a game. More than that, he was an expert at moving the ball. "Those crisp passes are the key to Isiah's becoming an instant leader," said John Mengelt, the Pistons' former radio

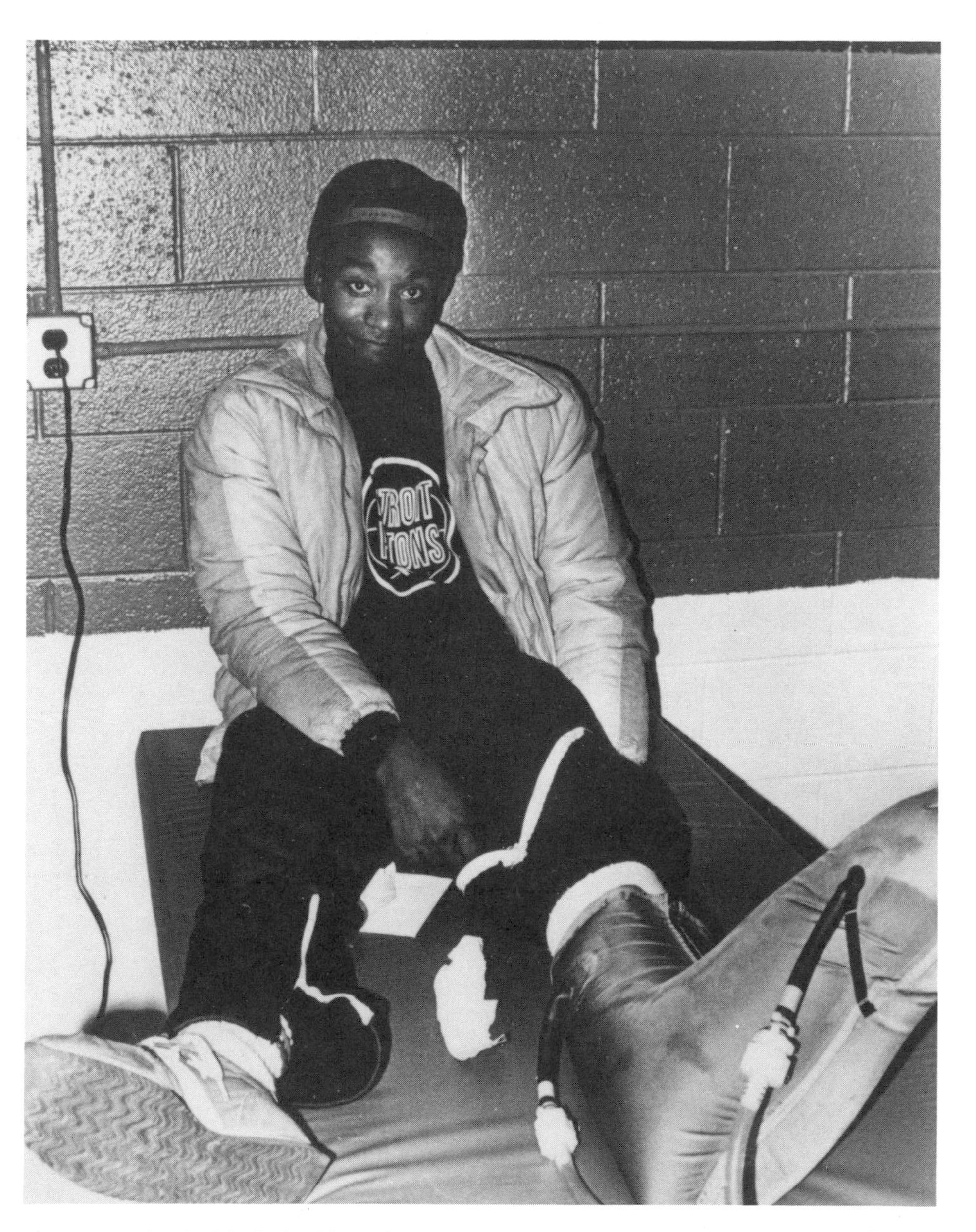

A sprained ankle during his rookie season with the Detroit Pistons kept Isiah out of action for ten games.

announcer. Thomas got a lot of points and assists, but fans liked him because he was fun to watch. "'Sparkle,' 'glitter,' 'pizzazz'—those words come to mind when I think of Isiah Thomas," said Pat Williams, the former general manager of the Philadelphia 76ers. "There is a certain joy he radiates on the court."

Isiah finished the 1981–82 season with 1,225 points—an average of 17 per game. He also had 565 assists. He was elected to the All-Rookie and All-Star teams. The Pistons won 39 games for third place in the Central Division of the Eastern Conference—their best finish in five years! During Thomas's first year in Detroit, the Pistons started putting together the team that would one day dominate the NBA. Vinnie "V. J." Johnson, a 6-foot 2-inch guard, was traded from the Seattle SuperSonics. Bill Laimbeer, a 6-foot 11-inch center, came from the Cleveland Cavaliers.

When his rookie season was over Isiah went back to

Isiah laughs after he and Magic Johnson fell to the floor at the Pontiac Silverdome.

Bloomington, Indiana to visit the campus with his girlfriend Lynn Kendall. He took her to the steps of the campus library. That was where they had met for their first date. Over the years Isiah had written her poems and given her flowers, but her favorite presents had always been Snickers candybars. When they got to the library steps Isiah asked her to close her eyes. "I have a surprise," he said.

Lynn thought he was teasing her. "Is it a Snickers?" This time it was not a candybar. Isiah handed her an engagement ring. It was his way of proposing marriage. A year later they were married and moved into a big house in Bloomfield Hills, a suburb of Detroit. Isiah had a gym built there so he would always have a place to practice.

Before the wedding Thomas played his second year with the Pistons. In the 1982–83 season Detroit was third with a 37–45 record. Thomas averaged 22.9 points a game and was again named to the All-Star team. That was Robertson's last year as coach. Jack McCloskey, the Pistons general manager, was getting impatient for a winning team. He fired Robertson and hired Chuck Daly—a former coach who had been working as a television commentator in Philadelphia, Pennsylvania.

Daly was not sure he could turn the lowly Pistons into contenders for the NBA championship. "I don't know how long I'm going to be here," he said. "I don't know if I can do a better job than Scotty Robertson. But . . . . we'll have some fun as we try to improve and see what happens.

The next year Thomas led Detroit to its first winning season in seven years. The Pistons won 49 and lost 33 games to finish second in the Central Division. This record qualified them for a playoff series against the New York Knicks.

The two teams split the first four games of the series. In the fifth game the Pistons trailed 106–98 with 1:57 to go. In the next 94 seconds Isiah popped in three jump shots, a layup, five free throws, and a three-pointer—16 points in 94 seconds! The game was now tied 114–114. Unfortunately Isiah's incredible performance was not enough. The Pistons lost in overtime 127–123.

In the 1984–85 season Isiah set the NBA record for assists—1,123. Detroit made the playoffs again, but did not get any further than the second round. This time they were stopped by Larry Bird and the Boston Celtics.

With his basketball skills, happy good looks, and winning personality, Isiah Thomas soon became one of the most popular sports personalities in Detroit. Everybody seemed to like him—especially McCloskey. After the 1984–85 season

Isiah talks with Piston coach Chuck Daly.

McCloskey gave Isiah a new contract. Isiah would now get more than a million dollars for each of the next ten years.

In the 1985–86 season the Pistons had their second 46–36 record in a row. But they were bumped off in the first round of the playoffs by the Atlanta Hawks.

During the off-season Isiah's face was a familiar one throughout the Detroit area. He wrote a weekly column for kids in the *Detroit Free Press.* He appeared at inner-city schools to tell young people to stay in school. And he made an anti-drug film *Just Say No.*

It was Isiah's idea to have a citywide "No Crime Day." For years Detroit had been plagued by heavy drug use and a high crime rate. Thomas hoped that if the city took a day to concentrate on the problem, perhaps the situation would improve. He convinced Mayor Coleman Young to set aside September 27, 1986 as "No Crime Day." Some people thought it was a silly idea, but that did not bother Thomas. "We accomplished the things we really wanted to," he said. "There were masses of people who organized themselves in block clubs and neighborhoods and communities to try to prevent crime."

Thomas's concern won the respect of NBA officials and opposing players throughout the league. He received the J. Walter Kennedy Citizenship Award for his community work, and he was elected president of the NBA Players Association.

When he was not playing basketball or doing community work, Isiah continued to keep his promise to his mother. He attended classes in Detroit and back in Bloomington. He still wanted to get his college degree.

But in the back of his mind was a dream he shared with all professional basketball players: he wanted his team to win an NBA championship. He had a plenty of individual honors. He had played in the All-Star game every year. And twice, in

1984 and 1986, he had been named the game's Most Valuable Player. But the Pistons had never finished higher than second in their conference and they had never made it past the second round of the playoffs.

Slowly the Piston lineup was improving. Rick Mahorn, a tough forward from the Washington Bullets, joined the team in 1985. This was the same year that Detroit drafted Joe Dumars, a 6-foot 3-inch guard. Adrian Dantley, a former NBA scoring champ, came a year later from the Utah Jazz. Also in 1986 Dennis Rodman, a 6-foot 8-inch forward, was picked up in the college draft. Isiah and his teammates hoped that soon they would bring the NBA Championship to Detroit.

Isiah jokes with comedian Billy Crystal before a benefit exhibition game.

Chapter 5

The Detroit Pistons sailed through the 1986–87 regular season with a 52–30 record—good enough for second place in the Central Division. In the first round of the playoffs, they mowed down the Washington Bullets three games to none.

Then in the first playoff game with the Atlanta Hawks, the Pistons led 109–108 with 19 seconds left. Isiah Thomas was fouled just as he dropped in a 19-foot jump shot. Isiah got the free throw, and Detroit won 112–111.

After a 115–102 Hawks' victory the teams stood at one game apiece. The third game, in Detroit, was tied 41–41 at the half. Then Bill Laimbeer, the Pistons' center, noticed Thomas was pumped up. "I could see it all coming," he said. "Isiah gets this gleam, this glow about him." During the next twelve minutes, Thomas scored 25 points. He also got 4 rebounds, 4 steals, and 2 assists. Each time he ran downcourt after a basket, he yelled at the Hawks. "You can't beat us here! This is our house!" He was right. The Hawks lost 108–99.

With time running out in the fourth game, Detroit trailed 88–87. Coach Chuck Daly called a timeout to make a plan.

There was no doubt who was going to get the ball. "Zeke was option 1, option 2, and option 3," said Laimbeer. Adrian Dantley threw the ball into Thomas, who was surrounded by John Battle and Antoine Carr. "He was smothered," said Laimbeer. The Hawks had their bodies between Isiah and the basket. "All of a sudden I just saw the ball coming over the top." Laimbeer said. Somehow Thomas had gotten off a shot. The ball swished the net, and Detroit won 89–88.

The same day Isiah's last-second basket sank Atlanta, Mary Thomas was in Bloomington, Indiana. She was picking up her son's diploma. He had kept his promise: he had graduated from college. "I'm thrilled to death!" Mary Thomas said. After the game she and her son talked on the phone. "She was excited, crying, happy, shocked, a lot of things," Isiah said. Of course, she was talking about his diploma. She was too excited to ask about the basketball game!

The Pistons' next playoff opponents were the Boston Celtics. After the first four games they were tied two games apiece. Then in the fifth game, with 17 seconds to go, Thomas sank another pressure jumper. Detroit was now up 107–106. Larry Bird stormed toward the basket for a pressure shot of his own, but Dennis Rodman blocked the ball. Bird fell to the floor and there was a scramble for the ball. It finally bounced off a Celtic and went out of bounds. The Pistons had possession with five seconds left.

Thomas prepared to pass the ball inbounds. A quick, crisp throw was needed. Instead Isiah lofted a soft, slow pass to Laimbeer. Bird quickly intercepted the ball. He then flipped it to teammate Dennis Johnson who was racing for the basket. Johnson's layup gave the Celtics a 108–107 victory. Isiah's mistake had given the game away.

Bird got 35 points in the next game, but Detroit could not be stopped this time. They won 113–105, setting up a seventh

Larry Bird led the Boston Celtics to a playoff victory over Detroit in 1987.

Adrian Dantley's injury helped seal the Pistons' fate in the 1987 NBA playoffs. Later he played for the Dallas Mavericks.

and final game. That match was a "classic." "It was hot in Boston Garden, about 98 degrees in the shade with no air conditioning," said Daly. "I perspired so much I ruined a good suit . . . . It was close, back and forth the whole way."

Late in the third period, however, misfortune struck the Pistons. Dantley and Vinnie Johnson dove for a loose ball under the Detroit basket. They banged heads and fell to the floor. Dantley was taken to a hospital with a concussion. "Johnson was useless the rest of the way," said Daly. His sore neck made it hard for him to play. With two of their best players gone, the Pistons were in trouble. Thomas's 25 points kept it close, but Detroit lost the game—and the series—117–114.

The Pistons were very disappointed. Their season was over. After the game Rodman got tired of hearing good things about Larry Bird. He said the Celtic star was overrated. Isiah agreed. "I think Larry is a very, very good basketball player, an exceptional talent," he said. "But . . . if he was black, he'd be just another guy."

Thomas later said he meant the comments as a joke. But by then a lot of people were mad. Many people believe that Bird is one of the finest players of all time. Isiah had been hot, tired, and frustrated. He quickly realized he had made a mistake. He apologized to Bird and explained what he had been trying to say. "What I was referring to was not so much Larry Bird, but the perpetuation of stereotypes about blacks. When Bird makes a great play, it's due to his thinking, and his work habits. It's all planned out by him. It's not the case for blacks. We never practice or give a thought to how we play . . . . Magic and Michael Jordan and me, for example, we're playing only on God-given talent . . . . while Larry's success is due to intelligence and hard work." After Isiah's explanation many athletes and reporters, both black and white, came to his defense. They agreed that every great athlete, no matter what his color, has to use his head and work hard.

The Pistons had come within a game of making it to the 1987 NBA finals. One year later they finally made it. First they won the Central Division with a 54–28 record. Then, after defeating Washington, Chicago, and Boston in the playoffs, Detroit had to face the defending champs—the Los Angeles Lakers.

That 1988 series brought Isiah up against Magic Johnson, one of his best friends. As soon as Isiah made it to the NBA, Magic said, "we became friends almost immediately because we shared a lot of the same experiences growing up . . . . The more we talked, the more we realized how much alike we were, how many secrets we shared." But playing each other for the title was going to be tough. "Here we were best of friends, but we were enemies for two weeks."

Thomas usually stayed at Johnson's home when the

Magic Johnson became one of Isiah's best friends in the NBA.

Pistons came to Los Angeles, but during the 1988 finals they stayed away from each other. Isiah said, "Magic had told me that even though we were friends, if I came down the lane trying to score, he'd slam me if he had to stop me." As Magic explained, "Once the ball went up, it was war."

The Pistons had never been in a finals before, but they were ready. When the first game began in Los Angeles, Isiah said, "We came out smoking—we were like a bunch of wild animals that had just been let out of their cage." Detroit won 105–93.

Magic was the one who was hot in the second game. He had 23 points, and the Lakers won 108–96. Then, back at the Silverdome, the Pistons lost again, 96–86. Late in the game Isiah fell on the court and bruised his back. He was in such pain that he spent the next two days in bed. But he still managed to show up for game four. In that game, as Thomas drove for the basket, Magic hit him with his elbow. Isiah shoved him back and for a second, it looked like the two friends might come to blows. Teammates separated them, and Detroit went on to win easily 111–86. The series was tied at two games apiece.

Before the next game Isiah watched his wife Lynn give birth to their first child, a son named Joshua Isiah. When the doctor said, "It's a boy!," Thomas cried. "I've never been happier in my life," he said.

In the next game Isiah was not too sharp. "I hadn't slept for four straight days and had too many things on my mind other than basketball." Los Angeles jumped to a 15–2 lead, and Daly put Thomas on the bench. Vinnie Johnson replaced him, scoring 16 points, and the Pistons won 104–94. One more victory and they would be the NBA champions.

Back in Los Angeles the Lakers led at the half 53–46. Isiah came out in the second half determined to take back the lead. He had 14 quick points, and it seemed like the Pistons were on their way to the title. But then on a fast break Isiah tripped over Michael Cooper. Isiah fell to the floor with a severely sprained ankle. It looked like he would have to spend the rest of the game on the bench.

But Thomas was not about to watch the championship slip away. Thirty-five seconds after he was taken out, he lied to Mike Abdenour, the Piston trainer. "Tell Chuck I'm ready to go back in," he said. Playing on one good leg, he scored 11 more points, giving him 25 points in the third quarter. This total was an NBA finals record. With only one quarter left, Detroit was leading 81–79. "He was out of this world," wrote Mike Downey, a columnist for the *Los Angeles Times*. "He

Isiah relaxes on the bench with Joe Dumars and Bill Laimbeer.

was making shots off the wrong foot, off the glass, off the wall."

The Pistons still led 102–101 with 14 seconds left, but then Laimbeer fouled Kareem Abdul-Jabbar, the greatest scorer in the history of professional basketball. The Forum crowd went wild as Jabbar sank both free throws. The Pistons could not score after that, and the Lakers won 103–102. The series was tied at three games all.

After the game Thomas said his ankle was as big as a basketball. He spent the next two days in the training facility of the Los Angeles Raiders, the National Football League team. The Raiders' trainers tried to bring the swelling down. Thomas could barely walk, but he started the final game. The Pistons led 57–52 at the half, but the Lakers outscored then 36–21 in the third quarter. Magic and his Los Angeles team finally won, 108–105, taking their second straight NBA championship.

Isiah did not have the title, but basketball fans all over the country were impressed by his skill, determination, and courage. Jack McCloskey showed his appreciation by giving Thomas a new contract worth $2 million a season.

Chapter 6

Nobody doubted that Isiah Thomas was earning the big money he was making with the Detroit Pistons. Magic Johnson knew that Isiah Thomas was a special athlete. "I love watching my buddy Isiah dribble the basketball," he said. "Rat-tat-tat-tat-tat-tat-tat-tat! Just like that. It sounds like a machine gun."

When Magic's Los Angeles Lakers play Isiah's Detroit Pistons, Johnson knows he must be prepared. "I just know Isiah's going to do something that'll make me look as though I don't know which way is up."

"Isiah is the most perfect point guard in the game today," said Don Nelson, coach of the Golden State Warriors. "There isn't anything Isiah can't do or doesn't do on the basketball court."

The point guard is the player who brings the ball upcourt. It is this player's job to set up the team's offense by shooting or passing the ball to a teammate. "When you get the ball," Thomas said, "you have to look for someone who is open. That's what basketball is all about—helping the team." He makes his job sound simple. "If the guy's open, then you kick him the ball," he said. "If he's not and you have the shot, then you have to take the shot . . . . To me it doesn't matter."

Thomas has always been known as a pressure player. When the Pistons need a basket, they give him the ball. On January 25, 1989, with 30 seconds left, Detroit was down 104–103 against Golden State. Only one man stood between Isiah and the game-winning basket—7-foot 6-inch Manute Bol, the tallest man in the NBA. Thomas threw the ball up and over Bol. It bounced once and went in. The Pistons won 105–104.

On January 27, the Cleveland Cavaliers led 80–79 with 13 seconds to go. Once again Daly decided that Isiah was the one who would take the shot. Thomas made his way to the baseline and let loose a jumper. This time the shot missed, and the Cavaliers won. Isiah finished the game with 22 points, but that did not matter. He had missed the big shot, and the Pistons had lost.

"It's great to be a hero and sink the game winner," Thomas wrote in his book *Bad Boys*, "but more importantly to me, I feel I'm strong enough to take the heat when I miss the last shot. I do know that I'm the one who wants to take that shot, make or miss."

Against the Denver Nuggets on March 6, things were close until Isiah got hot in the last quarter. He scored 15 points in the final ten minutes, and Detroit won 129–112. Five days later he could not be stopped against Philadelphia. He made 24 points in the fourth quarter—a regular-season Detroit record! The Pistons won 111–106.

Detroit played its worst basketball March 31 in Seattle. At halftime the SuperSonics led 69–46. The Pistons were getting blown away, and Isiah was mad. In the locker room he told his teammates, "If any of you guys quit, I'm personally going to kick your butt." The Pistons might be down by 23 points, but Thomas felt they were a good enough team to come back and win.

He was right. The Detroit defense tightened up and Seattle did not make a shot from the floor in the last ten minutes. The Pistons finally went ahead with a minute left. A Thomas jump shot clinched the game 111–108.

Just before the playoffs Isiah lost his temper and almost blew the entire season. The Pistons and the Chicago Bulls always play hard basketball against each other. Isiah had his hands full against Bill Cartwright, the Bulls' center. Cartwright's elbows had already caught Thomas twice that season, giving him stitches above both eyes.

On April 7 in Chicago, Cartwright was attempting to shoot when Thomas stole the ball. As Isiah took off Cartwright took a punch at him. Thomas turned around and punched back. The

Isiah wears goggles after a minor eye operation.

referees broke up the fight and both players were thrown out of the game.

In the locker room Isiah noticed that his left hand was swollen. The doctors said it was broken. The next day Isiah was wearing a splint. He was angry at Cartwright, but he was even angrier at himself. He had lost his temper and gotten into a fight. Now the doctors were telling him he might be out for the season. Isiah might have been angry, but he was hardly ready to give up. "Because I have worked so hard for so long, I was determined that an injury was not going to stop me from playing for a championship," he said later. Five days after the injury he was back in action, playing with just a protective glove on his broken hand.

The Pistons ended the 1988–89 regular season with their best record ever, winning 63 games and losing only 19. Detroit's first playoff opponents in 1989 were the Boston Celtics. The Pistons easily won the series in three straight games. Isiah played all three games though his hand was still bothering him.

Thomas was not his old self until the third game of the next series against the Milwaukee Bucks. That was the first time since his injury that he could shoot the ball left-handed. He scored 15 points in the third quarter as Detroit won 110–90. In the fourth game, with 20 seconds left and Detroit leading by two. Thomas sank a free throw to clinch the victory. The Pistons beat Milwaukee 96–94, taking the series four games to none.

Next the Pistons knocked off Michael Jordan and the Chicago Bulls, making themselves the Eastern Conference champions for the second year in a row. Then they took out the Los Angeles Lakers in four straight games to become the NBA champions.

One of the reasons for the Pistons' success was Mark

Aguirre, Isiah's old friend from Chicago. Halfway through the season he had been traded to Detroit from the Dallas Mavcricks for Adrian Dantley. When Aguirre heard about the trade, he said, "Great. It'll be great to join Isiah."

Isiah told his friend what the team expected. "First," he said, "you have to learn what it means to be a Piston. One thing it means is playing hard every minute of the game. There are no nights off on this team."

Aguirre worked hard to get the confidence of his new teammates. He averaged 15 points a game, but became better known for the smooth way he moved the ball to his teammates. After Aguirre joined the Pistons they won 30 of 36 regular season games.

When the 1989–90 season started the Pistons wanted to be the NBA champions once again. During a stretch in January and February, they won 25 games and lost only one. When the regular season ended they were again on top of the Central Division, this time with a 59–23 record. In the playoffs they dropped the Indiana Pacers in three straight games. Then they got by the New York Knicks four games to one.

Next it was time to once again face Michael Jordan and the Chicago Bulls. By then Jordan was probably the most famous athlete in America, but his team had never won a championship. After a pair of easy Detroit victories, Thomas had 62 points in the next two games. But Jordan dumped in 89, and Chicago won both games. Now the series was tied.

In the next game Aguirre saved the day, hitting eight of ten shots from the floor. Detroit won 97–83. But Jordan was strong in the sixth game, scoring 29 points and leading the Bulls to a 109–91 win. "We are more driven than ever to win this thing." Jordan yelled. The series was again tied, three games apiece. One game remained.

The Pistons finally ended the Bulls' dreams in the last

Isiah shoots over Michael Jordan.

game by winning 93–74. Isiah had 21 points. Jordan was disappointed but impressed. "They overwhelmed us," he said.

Now only the Portland Trail Blazers stood between Detroit and another NBA championship. In the first game the Pistons got into trouble. With seven minutes left they trailed by ten points. Coach Chuck Daly called a timeout. He pointed to Magic Johnson sitting in the stands and told Isiah. "Don't let Magic see you lose this game." That was all it took. Before play resumed, Thomas asked each of his teammates, "How badly do you want it?"

Then, as Daly explained, "Isiah got hot. He started throwing in everything, from everywhere. The place was bedlam and our players on the bench were going crazy. Isiah was throwing up unbelievable shots and everything was dropping." Thomas had 12 points in the last seven minutes. The Pistons took the lead and won 105–99.

The Trail Blazers won a 106–105 thriller in overtime before Detroit bounced back to take the third game 121–106. Joe Dumars was the Pistons' high scorer. As soon as the game was over, however, Dumars was told that his father had died after a long illness. Isiah stayed with him. Suddenly the game, the playoffs, and even the title did not seem very important. "It really puts everything in perspective," Isiah said. That night he and Dumars had a quiet dinner away from the fans and reporters.

Despite Dumars's personal tragedy the Pistons played another game two days later. Dumars scored 26 points, and Isiah was hot, too—hitting 22 points in the third quarter alone! Detroit led by as many as 16 points, but then it all fell apart in the final quarter. The Pistons got sloppy while the Trail Blazers got hot. Thomas lost the ball three times. Suddenly, with thirty seconds left, Portland had a one-point lead.

Once again it was Thomas who recovered from his

mistakes and came through when it counted. He had the ball in the corner with two men guarding him. The shot went up over their heads and through the hoop. As Daly said, "All those hours of working at the gym in his Bloomfield Hills home paid off." Detroit led 110–109.

Ten seconds later Isiah stole the ball from Terry Porter. He then passed it to Gerald Henderson who made an easy layup. The Pistons won 112–109 and led the series three games to one. They only needed one more win to clinch their second NBA championship in a row.

The next game was rough. Thomas was bumped hard and had to be taken out of the game with a bloody nose. Daly was afraid it was broken. Isiah wanted to play, but the bleeding would not stop. The Trail Blazers built a lead. With just two minutes left they were up 90–83. Finally the bleeding stopped, and Thomas went back in. Daly thought his team could still pull off a victory. "We have a lot of time," he told them. "We're a championship club."

Right away Vinnie Johnson dropped in a shot, took a foul, and made a free throw. The Portland lead fell to 90–86. Then the Trail Blazers missed a shot. Bill Laimbeer grabbed the rebound, and Thomas got the basket. Now the score was 90–88. Portland missed another basket, and Johnson scored again. Suddenly the game was tied.

With twenty seconds on the clock, Portland lost the ball out of bounds. Daly called a timeout. Isiah had a familiar idea for a championship-winning play. "Let me have it," he said. "If they double-team, I'll kick it to a shooter . . . . If not, I'll go in myself."

Thomas took the ball. When he was not double-teamed, he headed for the basket. Then Johnson's man, Jerome Kersey, left him to go after Isiah. Since Johnson was open Thomas threw him the ball. Johnson went high into the air and swished a short shot. Detroit had the lead 92–90. When Portland missed a shot at the buzzer, the Pistons had their second NBA championship.

Now there could be no question as to who was the dominant team in the NBA. The Pistons had won the title two years in a row. During those 1988–89 and 1989–90 seasons they had won 30 playoff games and lost only 7. Somebody asked Thomas if the second title was better than the first. "It was," he said, "because people doubted we could do it this time." He also had a prediction about the 1990–91 season. When Daly was thinking about retiring from coaching to become a television commentator, Isiah told him, "If you stay, we'll win three in a row." Daly decided to stay, and the Pistons went after another title.

President George Bush demonstrates ball control to Mark Aguirre, Bill Laimbeer, Vinnie Johnson, and Isiah at a White House ceremony.

But the 1990–91 season would prove to be a disappointing one for Detroit and a painful one for Thomas. In October he had a minor operation on his eyes. His own injured tear ducts were replaced by tubes. For a few days he wore goggles to protect his eyes so he could still play. Early in January he pulled a groin muscle. For a while the pain made it almost impossible for him to even pull on his socks. But Thomas kept playing.

In January his right wrist hurt so badly he had it examined by doctors. They told him he had been playing with a broken wrist. Still Thomas tried to keep playing. But finally, when the pain became too intense, he had to stop. After an operation he missed 32 games waiting for his wrist to heal. He was not able to return until just before the playoffs. In one of his first games back, he scored 26 points. His performance helped the Pistons beat the Chicago Bulls 95–91. "We're getting that same old magic back," he said as he soaked his wrist in ice water after the game.

Detroit split the opening two playoff games with the Atlanta Hawks. In the first half of the third game the Pistons fell behind 46–29. Then the Pistons stormed back to win 103–91, aided by Thomas's 19 points and Dumars's 30. The Hawks then took a 123–111 victory to force a decisive fifth game. In this game the Pistons looked like champions. Isiah led all scorers with 26 points, helping Detroit to win 113–81. The Pistons advanced to the next round against the Boston Celtics.

Throughout the playoffs Thomas continued to play with a splint on his injured right wrist. During the Atlanta series he had pulled his right hamstring muscle. Then late in Detroit's first playoff game against Boston. Dee Brown accidentally stepped on Isiah's right foot. Thomas fell to the court, his sprained foot yanked right out of his shoe! He had to be helped into the locker room, but Detroit still won 86–75. Teammate John Salley tried to joke about the injury. Sure,

Isiah watches the game from the bench while his wrist heals.

Isiah had problems with his right wrist, right hamstring and right foot, but "he has the whole left side to play with."

The sprained foot was bad enough that Thomas had to sit out the second game, which the Celtics won 109–103. "I can deal with most injuries," he said, "but when your feet hurt, you can't do squat." He tried to play in the next game, but only managed to score seven points as the Pistons lost 115–83. "I really shouldn't have played," he said. "The body can't overcome all these injuries."

Thomas sat out the fourth game to let his foot heal. In this game Aguirre scored 34 points, and the Pistons won 104–97. Isiah's body still ached, but his limp was gone so he came back for the fifth game. Detroit won again 116–111.

Then, despite the injuries, he put on his most thrilling performance of the season. The sixth game was tied 105–105 at the end of regulation play. Celtics Reggie Lewis and Ed Pinckney got quick baskets in overtime, and Boston led 109–105. With four seconds left on the shot clock the Pistons were still down 109–107. Thomas took the inbounded pass, dribbled to the right, and then released a long shot just in time. The shot buzzer went off as the ball banked off the backboard and through the net. Detroit now led 110–109.

Then, with 53 seconds left and the Pistons up by three, Boston's Brown tried to work his way under the basket for a shot. Isiah was all over him, guarding him so closely that Brown traveled. The Pistons got the ball. Thomas made two more jump shots before the game ended in a 117–113 Detroit victory. The Pistons won the series, four games to two.

With the Celtics out of the way, it was time to once again take on Chicago. Michael Jordan and the Bulls won the first game 94–89. "That was a well-played game," Isiah said. "The Bulls did everything well." Then Jordan got 35 points, and Chicago won again 105–97. "We're playing like we're more hungry than they are," said the Chicago superstar. The Pistons were digging a hole.

In the third game Jordan's 33 points helped bury Detroit 113–107. And after a 115–94 Chicago victory in the fourth game, their quest for a third NBA title was over. The Bulls had finally beaten the Pistons in a playoff series. For the first time in four years Detroit would not be in the NBA finals. As the last game was ending, Isiah and his teammates hugged each other on the sidelines. The Pistons' championship days were over, but there would not be any excuses. "No television, no refs, don't blame anything else," Thomas said. "They beat us because they were the better basketball team." Jordan and the Bulls went on to defeat the Los Angeles Lakers to take their first NBA championship.

After the 1990–91 season Isiah Thomas was only 30 years old. He figures he still has a few more years left with the Pistons. After that maybe he will stay in basketball and coach younger players. Or maybe he will go to law school. He has also expressed an interest in being an actor. In fact, he has already discussed the possibility of an acting career with executives of Touchstone Pictures.

Isiah's old friend and high school coach Gene Pingatore is sure he will be a success after his playing career is over. "Someday Isiah's going to walk away from basketball and do even more important things in society—television, Hollywood, politics, who knows? He has the ability to do whatever he wants to do."

Coach Pingatore first met Isiah Thomas when he was an eighth grader living in the slums of Chicago. Since then he has watched him come a long way. "I'm really proud of his accomplishments, but I'm more proud of the way he turned out. He's a caring, responsible adult. He's always done the right thing. He's always been a super person."

Career Statistics

COLLEGE

YEAR	TEAM	GP	FG%	REB	PTS	AVG
1979-80	Indiana University	29	.510	116	423	14.6
1980-81	Indiana University	34	.554	105	545	16.0
	TOTAL	127	.613	1314	2669	21.0

NBA

YEAR	TEAM	GP	FG%	REB	AST	STL	BLK	PTS	AVG
1981-82	Detroit	72	.424	209	565	150	17	1225	17.0
1982-83	Detroit	81	.472	328	634	199	29	1854	22.9
1983-84	Detroit	82	.462	327	914	204	33	1748	21.3
1984-85	Detroit	81	.458	361	1123	187	25	1720	21.2
1985-86	Detroit	77	.488	277	830	171	20	1609	20.9
1986-87	Detroit	81	.463	319	813	153	20	1671	20.6
1987-88	Detroit	81	.463	278	678	141	17	1577	19.5
1988-89	Detroit	80	.464	273	663	133	20	1458	18.2
1989-90	Detroit	81	.438	308	765	139	19	1492	18.4
1990-91	Detroit	48	.435	160	446	75	10	776	16.2
	TOTAL	764	.456	2840	7431	1552	210	15130	19.8

Index